SHOWBIZ

presents

A PARENT'S GUIDE TO MANAGING SHOWBIZ KIDS

PAMELA WARNER

ShowBiz Consulting 411 presents
A PARENT'S GUIDE TO MANAGING SHOWBIZ KIDS

ISBN # 979-8-9887860-0-9 (Paperback)
ISBN # 979-8-9887860-1-6 (Ebook)

Author: Pamela Warner
Interior Book & Cover Design: Velin@Perseus-Design.com
Cover Photography: Bradford Rogne
Publisher: Power2Excel Agency, LLC

Printed in the United States of America.

PRAISE FOR A PARENT'S GUIDE TO MANAGING SHOWBIZ KIDS ...

"A Parent's Guide To Managing ShowBiz Kids" by Talent Manager Pamela Warner of Warner Management is a manual for everyone with children in show business or wanting to be in the entertainment industry. With a career spanning decades and a flawless track record with her successful son, Malcolm-Jamal Warner, mother and Manager Pamela Warner opens the golden doors to the industry's most coveted secrets in this unparalleled masterpiece. This manual is not just a guide; it's your golden ticket.

Ms. Warner leaves nothing out in this priceless manual about what a parent with a child or children in the business must know to succeed in the entertainment business and have a lasting and loving relationship with their child when they are no longer underage. Ms. Warner bares her soul in her easy-to-read and follow guide for parents. And, when you thought this manual couldn't get any more comprehensive, she surprises you with an entertainment glossary of terms that seamlessly decipher the industry jargon and allows you to navigate through showbiz intricacies like a seasoned professional. Owning this book is a must for all parents of kids in show business.

Lola! Love, MS, LOAcc, NLP, DTM, Speech Coach
www.LHBconsultcoach.com

"A Parent's Guide to Managing Showbiz Kids" is a MUST-HAVE for any parent looking to get their child into the business of show! This handbook is loaded with pertinent and necessary information that will make any journey into show business smoother for both the parent and the child.

Pamela also discusses the soul-searching and critical questions one must ask to honestly determine whether getting into show business is a desire of the child or the desire of the parent and how important it is to know the difference.

I recommend this handbook as required reading for any parent who enrolls their child into any acting class!

Adrienne Fishe
International Entertainer / Singer / Actor

Pamela Warner, friend and exceptional Personal Manager, has written an in-depth, concise guide for any parent who wants to know the ins and outs of what and how to properly manage, guide, and direct their child into the world of show business.

It takes more than pure providence or being in the right place at the right time to build a successful career in the entertainment industry. Pamela had no guidance or knowledge of the business, but her vision, belief, and faith in her son's talent helped steer her way into a respected career. Without the proper knowledge, training, preparation, and unstoppable dedication and determination, talent alone will not get you there.

Pamela and her son, Malcolm, shared those qualities. This marvelous handbook will take you step-by-step along the arduous path as you pursue the intricate journey of being/becoming a Personal Manager.

Micheal Cushman/Former Personal Manager
COPM President/Producer

Pamela Warner has been a devoted producer, manager, mother, and faithful friend for decades. She is loyal to her people. In "A Parent's Guide to Managing Showbiz Kids," you'll find a brilliant and necessary toolbook to guide, empower, and support you and your child's journey as you embark upon and learn to maintain an acting career successfully. There is no better way to spend your time and energy in gauging the litmus test of required discipline, motivation, and responsibility for safeguarding your child's career and finances. Ms. Warner has eloquently managed her son Malcolm's career on an undeniable road from glory to glory. All the wisdom and reference you'll ever need are here and clear. It is my honor to be a part of this magnificent debut!

Hilda Boulware
Actor, Author, and Children's Social Worker

When relocating to California from Indiana in 2016, my goal was for my two children and me to prosper in an acting career. Reading "A Parent's Guide to Managing Showbiz Kids" helped tremendously in accomplishing our goal.

The guide taught me the ins and outs of the industry and familiarized me with laws and terminology. Since 2019, we have continued to excel as background actors and humbly thank Ms. Pam Warner for sharing her passionate gift as a writer and parent management experience.

Taja Pryor, Screenwriter
Inglewood, California

After reading Pamela Warner's book, "A Parent's Guide to Managing Showbiz Kids," I was very impressed with how detailed and informative she presents from A-Z the hows of getting kids into Show business. I have had my talent agency for ten years. When interviewing kids and their parents to possibly sign with my Agency, they must understand that this is a business. "A Parent's Guide to Managing Showbiz Kids" is a must-read for anyone trying to make it in show business. I highly recommend Pamela Warner's book.

Diana Sellers, Owner
Nharmony Casting & Talent Management

If you want guidance from someone who has walked the path, has years of experience, and has managed an extraordinary career, you're in the right place. "A Parent's Guide To Managing Showbiz Kids" is THE expertise that will lead you in the right direction. Period.

Vernice Armour | Entrepreneur, Author
America's First Black Female Combat Pilot

Pamela Warner's "A Parent's Guide To Managing Showbiz Kids" is a must-have for parents/guardians who are assisting their child along the showbiz journey. As a former child actor, my mother and I learned some of the pitfalls by trial and error. It would have been great to have a book like this detailing what to be aware of to have a successful career in this industry. Depending on the age of your child, some of the chapters would be great to read along with them. This book offers many life lessons outside of the show business industry as well. Impressive!

Claude Brooks
Actor/Producer

Knowledge is power, and in this book, Pamela Warner provides the key elements to success. She arms you with the knowledge that is needed and necessary to be successful in this entertainment business. Kudos Pam!

Dawn Carter, Producer

ACKNOWLEDGMENT

This book would not have happened were it not for my son, Malcolm-Jamal Warner, and his desire to become an actor at eight years old. Being the mother that I was, I knew this effort would require my total support and involvement. While acting as a career choice was absolutely not on my radar, his desire to become an actor meant I had to become his manager.

This journey was a huge learning curve. Because of that experience, I can share this information with other parents who find themselves in the role of manager to protect their child/children and assist in making their children's dreams come true in a safe and healthy way. I have grown tremendously and learned so much. I have also had a life I would otherwise not have had. And I am deeply grateful for my son having a dream. Malcolm, there are not enough *Thank You's* for your support, love, and encouragement to write this book. You are my rock, my foundation, my world.

To Bill and Camille, thank you from the bottom of my heart for your kindness, graciousness, inclusion, guidance, and ongoing support. Bill, your casting decision changed the projectory of our lives and made a young boy's dream come true. Without the both of you, this book could not have been written.

There were also those souls; I like to call them angels, who held me up, pushed me forward, and encouraged me to write this book.

To Joya Wesley, who graciously did the very first edits. She named me the coma queen as I wrote as I spoke, but I needed to try a different method to write a book people could read. I will forever be indebted to Dr. Sharon Seigel, who generously gave her time, expertise, and care to do all developmental edits freely and fully. She was there for me even when I came up with additional chapters.

To Apryl Brown, while no longer with us in this dimension, continued to whisper, "There is someone out there who needs to hear what you have to say." Apryl was the first person to say that to me and continued to whisper to me from the other side, supporting me with my dream. She has been relentless from the other side.

To Vernice Armour, who, for too many years, pulled, pushed, and cajoled me to get out of my own way and tell the story.

ACKNOWLEDGMENT

To Dorothy Randall Gray, who just asked simple questions that produced huge "aha" moments for me.

To Dorothea Barlow, thank you for your never-ending love and encouragement. To Adrienne Fishe, an immense thank you for your keen eye, care, and support.

Lola! Love was a treasure trove of information, referrals, and support. She is also a mother who managed her son, so she knew my journey very well. To Valerie Yaro, historian/archivist from the communications department of SAG-AFTRA, who, while under an active strike, took her time to research information on child actors to ensure the information on child actors and the union was true and accurate.

To Adam Griffin and Justin Baxter, who cheered me on, providing critical information and support from beginning to end. And to the "Book Doula," Valerie McDowell, who assisted me in the birth of this book.

And to all of you not mentioned here, who supported me with kind words of encouragement and support, and there were many, I thank you from the bottom of my heart.

CONTENTS

FOREWORD

Let me be the first to say that *A Parent's Guide To Managing Showbiz Kids* is indeed long overdue. It was the book my mother could have used in 1981 when first dipping our toes into the world of television. When my mother put me in a community theater workshop, becoming a famous actor was the last thing on her mind. She was looking for anything extra-curricular that would keep my interest and keep me from hanging out in the neighborhood where trouble easily found kids, whether or not they were looking for it.

Like many of you, a woman who did not groom her son to be a showbiz kid wrote this handbook. So consider yourself lucky that there's not a lot of deprogramming you need to do. I consider myself incredibly lucky that my mother, armed with only her instinct, good sense, discernment, and sometimes even fear, could navigate the treacherous waters that the entertainment industry can be for children and adults alike, with our hearts, souls, and minds very much intact. During my teenage years on one of the most successful shows in television history, my mother mentally equipped me for life after teenage stardom. She helped shape my vision for longevity in this business, and 30 years after "The Cosby Show," I have worked consistently, and my craft has grown exponentially.

Given our 40 years of being in this business of entertainment, to say that Pamela Warner knows a lot is an understatement. *A Parent's Guide To Managing Showbiz Kids* will help those who aren't knowledgeable about the business but wish to begin a career. It offers practical advice from her experience working with agents, managers, casting directors, educators, accountants, lawyers, and other child advocates on a range of topics pertinent to youngsters. And though the industry has changed dramatically from my days as a child performer, the information here is timeless. While no one book can cover everything, this handbook is one of the best supplements available to a lifestyle that already promotes a child's best interest, written by a mother and manager — not a Momager —who always put her son's best interest before her ego.

MALCOLM-JAMAL WARNER
Actor-Director-Poet-Musician

INTRODUCTION

In the 40 years I have spent in the entertainment industry, I have found that parents just do not know how or where to get started and generally do not have an understanding of the industry. There are so many aspects of the business that parents often get lost, discouraged, or victimized. This handbook is written as a guide and reference to answer the many questions they might have and provide the information parents need to successfully manage their children's careers.

I have designed this handbook especially for the parent(s) who desire to have their children work in the entertainment industry. It is written for the parent who, just like me in the beginning, has no idea what steps to take and how to take them. While my experience is not the typical experience of many parents, this handbook still holds valuable information.

I will share with you everything I have learned over my four decades in the field.

This handbook will cover, ask, and answer many questions parents may have as they embark on this journey of managing their children in the entertainment industry.

CHAPTER 1

THE RELUCTANT PARENT MANAGER

My journey into show business was a little different from most parents. Usually, it is either the desire of the parent to put their children in show business or the desire of the child. For me, it was neither. My focus was to provide some sort of extra-curricular activity for my child. My son Malcolm was in Little League baseball, and he hated it. He tried basketball, and he hated that too. A friend suggested putting him in a local children's theater group. She was friends with the theater director, Gary Veney. I didn't feel I had anything to lose, and it sounded interesting. I met with the director, signed Malcolm up, and scheduled his audition. He won his audition and became a member of the Inglewood Playhouse.

Malcolm totally embraced the theater and the work. He had finally found something that truly engaged him. He was totally committed. He said to me after their first production, after he took his first curtain call, that this was what he wanted to do for the rest of his life. And from that evening until today, he has worked as an actor.

As a parent, I was satisfied because I had found that extra-curricular activity that I felt was necessary for my child. I believed that children needed to learn how to prioritize their time. They needed to have other challenges besides going to school and coming home, doing homework, and going outside to play. I have always thought that children have a great capacity at an early age to learn discipline, commitment, and focus. And I believe I have been proven correct. In addition to Malcolm's responsibilities as a member of the theater group, he still had academic responsibilities and household responsibilities. And to his credit, he fulfilled them all with flying colors. There was not much wiggle room. He had to accomplish all of his academic responsibilities and household responsibilities before he could go to the theater. No matter how close they may have been to the opening night of one of their productions, it was mandatory that his other commitments were completed first.

It may sound harsh, but I had no other way to test his commitment and real desire to become an actor. His focus and discipline propelled him over the hurdles that I set before him. Please understand, I was not preparing him for life as an actor but for life as a responsible human being. Being in show business was the farthest thing from my mind. I just wanted him to have an extra-curricular activity to which he could commit.

An agent approached me during the run of his first production. She had her own agency and wanted to sign him. I was in my last year of study for an undergraduate degree in speech communications, and I was not interested. It was a huge time commitment for me just to get him back and forth to the playhouse, let alone find time to take him on auditions. So I said no. It was more important for me to complete my education so I would be better able to provide for my child. At that time, Malcolm would soon be entering junior high school, and I wanted to make sure I could provide all he would need. That was my focus.

The next season, there was another production. The same agent approached me again. This time I considered it. I had earned my BA and completed my education. I had started a small catering business, so my time was my own. I took her up on the offer, signing Malcolm to her agency. For me, it was still an extra-curricular activity for him, and I was pleased that Malcolm was sticking with it. However, show business was still not a part of my vision.

Shortly after signing, Malcolm began to book. He had several television shows under his belt while still being involved with the Inglewood Playhouse. And then the big one came along, *The Cosby Show*. After Malcolm was cast in this show, it was clear this was now serious and we were both definitely in show business, whether I wanted to be or not.

Once that contract was signed, it gave new meaning to the term on-the-job training. While there was so much I didn't know, I knew I needed to learn what I didn't know really fast. Unfortunately, there was no one to help guide me. I had no connection with other parents who may have been managing their children. There were no resources. There was no internet to Google how to do this. All I had were my instincts, my degree in Speech Communications - which provided me with training in listening and being intuitive about what was said to me - and a fierce commitment to protect my child at all costs.

The not knowing was the scariest part. I did not know if the decisions I had to make would be career-enhancing or career-damaging. I just did not know. But with my focus being on the safety and protection of my child, I was confident that whatever decisions I made would be in Malcolm's best interests.

CHAPTER 2

WHY DO YOU WANT TO DO THIS?

The motivation for writing this handbook comes from those scary moments I experienced. I don't want other parents to be as afraid as I was. I want to empower parents. When you are empowered, you make decisions from a place of confidence, understanding, and knowledge, not fear.

Those of you on the cusp of making the decision to enter the world of show business are fortunate to have the luxury of being able to research beforehand. The internet is a wonderful thing in this instance. While this handbook is not the seminal publication for parents in show business, it is my story and includes observations, experiences, and information that I have gathered over a span of 40 years. I want to share it all with you.

One of the very first things you should do if you are considering entering show business is to ask yourself WHY? Why do you want to do this? What is your motivation? How you answer this question will surely determine your success or failure as a parent managing a child or children in show business.

It is absolutely imperative that you are clear that this journey is not for you but for your child. You must do your inner research and be sure you are not trying to serve an unmet need of your own. You must be crystal clear this is something your child wants to do. The industry is full of parents who want a show business career more than their children do. There are those parents who, at some time in their lives, wanted to be child actors, and for whatever reason, it just did not happen for them. So they become determined their children will be actors at any cost.

The poor child is helpless in this scenario. Children want to please, so they will go along with what their parents want. And that can be damaging to both the child and the parent.

There are several ways to determine if this is really what your child wants to do. Community theater is a great way to start. Locate children's theater groups in your area. You will be able to determine if your child really wants to do this by how the child participates in the group.

- Is the child focused?
- Does the child enjoy learning about theater?
- Does your child wholeheartedly participate?
- Is there eagerness to be a part of the group?
- Is the child's interest and enthusiasm sustained?
- Has he or she embraced the discipline to learn his or her lines?
- Is the child fully present?

Only you, as a parent, can determine this. You know your child, and you can evaluate if this is really something that your child wants to do and if they will stick to it. This also applies to dance and music.

Also, you should check in with your child. Ask them directly, "Are you really enjoying this? Do you like the things that you are doing at dance/music/theater class?" Your child will let you know if you are in it for the long haul or if you need to move on and find them some other interests.

Please make sure this is truly something the child wants to do. When parents with unmet needs push for a child to be an actor, dancer, or musician, it becomes about the parent and what the parent wants, and not what's good for the child or what the child may want. So take your time and evaluate closely whether you are on the right path with your child.

CHAPTER 3

Do You Have the Time and Energy?

Once you have determined and wish for your child to go into show business, the next step is to evaluate whether you have the time and energy to do this. You will need lots of both. You almost always have to be "on call." Audition hours will vary, and there is never a set schedule. When casting children, casting directors are sensitive to the fact that children are in school. They try to set auditions for school-age children toward the end of the school day. On rare occasions, you will have to take your child out of school for an audition.

When an agent calls you for an audition, will you be able to drop everything and get the child to the audition? If you are not available, will you have a reliable backup to get your child to the audition? Do you have reliable transportation? If you are a working parent, will your boss be OK with you leaving early or at midday in order to get your child to that audition? I was very fortunate during those early years because I had my own business and could schedule my time around Malcolm's auditions. But the commitment was the same, requiring me to get him to the auditions on time in front of the casting directors. Once you have decided to involve your child in show business, you simultaneously commit to being available. It is a huge commitment. But remember, you are helping your child make their dreams come true.

Another issue to think about, if it applies, is the other children in your home. How do you split your time between your showbiz kid and your other children? The showbiz child will take up an inordinate amount of your time. There will be a lot of attention focused on that showbiz kid. How do you balance your time with your other children? What if your other children have special interests? You also must be present for them. This is why it is necessary to have a backup. Perhaps there is a family member you can rely on when you have a time conflict. A backup must be in place for this to run smoothly. Looking back, I feel fortunate I only had one child. I believe it would have been quite difficult, particularly as Malcolm's career began to flourish, to have had another child or children needing my attention. You don't want jealousies to develop or siblings to feel left out or not as important as the showbiz sibling. This is a juggling act that I am grateful to have escaped. However, I give my whole-hearted support to those parents who find themselves in this situation.

CHAPTER 4

THE AGENT

When you recognize the need for an agent, you have already asked yourself the hard questions and made the commitment. You are feeling confident this is the journey you want to take with your showbiz kid. Now you need an agent! There are many agents and agencies to choose from. Just do a Google search to see how many there are. Do your research and determine which agency you feel will be a good fit for you and your child. If you know other parents who have children in show business, ask them for referrals. You will have to shop the agencies. What I mean by "shop" is that you will meet with the ones you have identified that will be of interest to you. They will interview you and your child, and you will interview them. You will like some, but they may have a conflict, such as another actor that is too similar to your child. Or you may not like them, but they really want to sign your child. Always go with your intuition and what your gut tells you. You can read their reviews, but what do you feel? It's okay to be wanted by an agency, but it is more important you feel safe and that your child will be safe.

Malcolm's first agent, Miriam Baum, at the time, owned a small boutique agency, Artists First. She had seen him in the first production at the Inglewood Playhouse and wanted to sign him to her agency. But it was just not the right time for me. My focus was not on show-business. My focus was on completing my education.

The following year, there was a second production. It was clear by then that Malcolm was thoroughly convinced he wanted to be an actor. As a parent, I was happy I had found that extra-curricular activity I desired for my son. Miriam approached me again, wanting to sign Malcolm to her agency. By this time, I had earned my degree, and my time was my own. I really liked Miriam, so I agreed. I was now set and ready to start this show-business journey.

An agent's primary function is to find work for your child, who becomes his or her client. The agent basically functions as an employment agency, and the agent must be licensed by the state of California. The agent pitches the clients to casting directors, who then present the clients to the directors and producers, who then hire your child. In exchange for finding work, the agent is paid a commission. Usually, it will be 10 percent of the gross income. This number is not written in stone. It can be any amount that is negotiated and agreed upon between you and the agent. The industry standard is 10 percent, and most agents will not go below this amount. Please keep in mind that there should be no upfront fees to represent your child. The agent is only paid a commission of the gross amount of your child's earnings and is paid only when the child is paid. There are many scammers out there and if you are asked for any upfront monies, run.

An agent can be very valuable in the career of an actor. When you start out, the agent you sign with is part of the developmental stage of your child's career. Some agents are very hands-on, and some are not.

However, you as the parent must develop a working relationship with the agent. The agent is the point person and negotiates salaries and contracts in order to get the best deal for the client, your child. They will also look for opportunities to advance your child's career through the projects for which he or she recommends. It was Miriam Baum who submitted Malcolm for *The Cosby Show* and who negotiated the deal.

Actors can go from agency to agency, trying to find the right fit for them and their career. I have been very fortunate in this area. As with most actors, there is a time in their career that they move on to other agencies. We were not the exception. Our next stop was with the iconic William Morris Agency, the leader in the industry for many years with offices around the world. The William Morris Agency had a very long and wonderful history. (Unfortunately, the agency was merged with Endeavor in 2009.) Norman Brokaw, who ran the agency for more than 50 years, signed Malcolm himself. William Morris was Malcolm's home for close to 20 years.

Around 2007, rumors began that William Morris was going to be bought/merged with Endeavor. So we left before we were folded into an agency where there was no relationship or history. Our next stop was with Abrams Artist Agency, another iconic talent agency. We were assigned to Justin Baxter, who exemplifies an agent who knows how to move an actor to the next step and expand a career. Justin was hands-on with clients. Malcolm's career flourished under his leadership and guidance.

The projects he has put Malcolm up for have been stepping stones to the next level of success. And while Justin guided Malcolm's career, his own career flourished, becoming Vice President and Partner at A3 Artists Agency, formerly known as Abram Artist Agency. Justin has since left A3 and is now a talent manager with Vault Entertainment.

It is important to remember that the agent works for your child. Not the other way around. Sometimes, the agent and parent forget this fundamental dynamic. You always have the right and responsibility to ask questions and to be heard.

Many agents, particularly those dealing with parents, can be a bit condescending. However, the agent often has to deal with parents who are anxious, obnoxious, or nervous, which can make their job difficult. Regardless, never forget that you have the last word as the parent. The agent cannot book a job or negotiate a contract without your consent. You will always have the prerogative to accept or reject a deal, project, or job presented to you. Many parents do not understand this. The parent is totally responsible for all decisions regarding the child's career. The agent cannot and should not enter into any agreement without your consent. It is the agent's responsibility to discuss all contracts, inquiries, auditions, and all things related to your child's career with you first before any action is taken.

This is an unfamiliar world for most parents. There will be new terms and phrases. If there is something you do not understand, ask and continue to ask until you thoroughly understand what the agent is communicating to you. This becomes essential in regard to contracts. Unless you are prepared to hire a lawyer, then you must do some on-the-job training. Fully understand everything you can about that contract. But whether you understand the contract or not, it is a binding document and may have clauses within it that may not be favorable to your child in the long run. It is up to you as a parent to have a working understanding of every word of that contract. If you do not have the time, or if you find it too difficult to understand, then it is advisable to hire an attorney who specializes in contracts. We will discuss attorneys in a later chapter. The idea here is to protect your child as best you can. This is a learning process for you and your child. And yes, you will make mistakes. But what is most important is that you gain as much information and understanding of the industry and the process of becoming an actor as possible.

CHAPTER 5

THE MANAGER

Like most businesses, in order for your child's career to grow and succeed, there needs to be planning. This is an essential component of all businesses. Being in show business is not much different from other businesses. You are running a business, and the business is entertainment, and the most valuable asset in that business is your child. You need to have a plan and a goal about where you want your child's career to go. You can do this planning yourself or you can hire an experienced manager who knows how to guide and shape careers. Finding a manager is a lot like finding an agent. You can do Google searches and you can ask other parents who are also in the business. Agents frequently work with managers and are also a good source of referrals.

There is a difference between an agent and a manager. Although from time to time their duties can and do overlap, agents must be licensed and are therefore regulated by the government. Managers are not required to be licensed.

An agent can procure work, obtain auditions, and administrate contracts. Some agents will do career planning, some won't. The role of the manager is to develop and guide your child's career. The fee for a manager is usually 10 percent of the gross income. Although it is the same for the agent, the manager is more hands-on with your child's career. Managers cannot broker deals for your child. They can and do work closely with the agent in terms of negotiating, but they cannot negotiate deals. Only the licensed agent can do this.

As in any other business, good management is a key to success. The goal and focus of a good manager is to guide and advise you and your child on career opportunities. The manager will always be on the lookout for opportunities. He or she will present you with opportunities and discuss with you the positive and negative aspects of each. This gives you the parent information needed for you to make wise choices for your child's career.

Managers, for the most part, have closer and more personal relationships with their clients. All managers are not the same, just as all clients are not the same. Some clients may need more hands-on attention, while others are more independent. Managers are more day-to-day as they communicate and interface with the agent for follow-ups on auditions and feedback from the casting directors.

I chose to step into the management position myself. I felt I was the best person for the job. It was quite difficult at first because I had no information about what to do. There was a lot I did not know. But I was committed to protecting my child at all costs. I relied on my gut instincts and what I thought would be best for Malcolm. In the beginning, I was overly cautious at times because I knew there was so much I did not know. But the more time I spent learning and doing, the more confident and relaxed I became in managing my son's career.

I sincerely believe that parents can be the best managers. for their children.

As parents, you know your children, their wants, their needs, what they like, and what is best for them. You know your children better than anyone else. The very best parent for the job has no unmet needs or hidden agenda and has a clear focus on the welfare of the child, is enthusiastic, and willing to learn and apply that knowledge for the benefit of their child.

Although I was putting in the day-to-day work as Malcolm's manager, I did not take what was due to me. Don't make that mistake. Your time and energy deserve compensation. You are entitled to the 10 percent commission due to any other manager. If you choose to co-manage, then that will be a discussion with the additional manager you bring in. How those commissions are split will be decided between you and the other manager.

Please note that at any time you feel uncomfortable or feel that the agent or manager that you have chosen is not working out for you, even though you have signed a contract/agreement with that agent, agency or manager, you can still leave. However, understand that commissions will still be owed to that agent, agency, or manager for the duration of the show or theatrical project on which your child may be working. Agents and managers want to be paid for their work, so a new agent, agency or manager will very rarely be willing to sign your child, knowing that the commissions will go to the former agent, agency, or manager. So, it behooves you to make sound decisions when signing with an agent, agency, or manager.

Currently, there is extensive information available for the parent/manager to access. You don't have to do this as blindly as I did, which is the reason I am writing this handbook. I never want any parent to be as uninformed as I was. I want to empower parents to manage their children with confidence, without fear of doing the wrong thing. As long as you have the welfare of your child as your focus and goal, you are not likely to go wrong.

CHAPTER 6

THE BUSINESS MANAGER

Once you've gotten acclimatized to the business and things are going fairly smoothly, your showbiz kid is booking regularly, and the checks are coming in, you will now need a business manager! A good business manager will help you manage the income your showbiz kid is earning. The business manager makes sure the proper deductions are taken out and that taxes are prepared and paid in a timely and orderly fashion. Yes, your child will now be a taxpayer. It is just as important that your child pay taxes on earned income as it is for you. The IRS will come after your child, just like they will come after you if taxes are not paid. The IRS does not distinguish between an adult or a child. The business manager will know what expenses can be deducted and which ones cannot. Since actors have expenses that average working people do not have, it is very important to have someone who is knowledgeable in tax preparation as it relates to the entertainment industry.

Another aspect of having a business manager is financial planning for your child's future. A good business manager will work with you to develop a plan. There are many avenues for saving and growing the money your child is earning. There are trust funds, stocks, bonds, and mutual funds. A good business manager will explore with you investment strategies that will be of benefit to your child.

I obtained a business manager in the second year of *The Cosby Show*. At that time, there were several high-profile cases of child actors whose parents had not taken care of their earnings and were broke. I was determined I would not be one of those parents. My son would not be able to say his mother took or mismanaged his money. So I was very motivated to make sure his earnings were protected. I hired the firm DeBlois, Mejia & Company. Richard DeBlois, who founded the company, retired several years ago and left the business in the capable hands of Wayne Mejia.

Richard and Wayne felt that the best way to protect Malcolm's earnings was to establish a company through which the income flowed, defined as a Loan Out company. A Loan Out Company, sometimes referred to as a Loan Out Corporation, is often used by entertainment professionals.

That person is then employed by the corporation and the corporation then loans out the services of the entertainment professional. There are benefits to this, but there are also additional requirements that are necessary to have a Loan Out corporation. Your business manager should be able to assist you in deciding which route to take. But as always, do your research!

We were now truly in show business. The company required regular financial meetings to discuss how the company was operating. I firmly believed Malcolm should also be involved in these meetings. I wanted to be absolutely transparent about his finances, so I insisted he attend these meetings with me. I thought it best that he participated in those meetings as well in case anything untoward happened. Whether he understood what was going on was immaterial to me. He would never be able to say he was not made aware of the operation of his company. I know it sounds like a lot to put on a 14-year-old, but I was terrified of being accused of mismanagement of his money. Of course, he hated attending these meetings, but my goal was also to establish financial responsibility on his part. These meetings were not fun. They were all about the numbers and excruciatingly boring for a teenage boy. I didn't care. I felt I was doing my part as a responsible parent and manager. For many years, I, along with Richard and Wayne, ran those meetings, asked the questions, signed documents, and did the financial planning for Malcolm's financial future.

Those meetings still occur today. The only difference is that now Malcolm runs those meetings. I am always so proud to see how involved he is. He asks all the right questions and makes good financial decisions. If I had not involved him as early as I did, I don't believe he would have had the ability to fully understand how his money works or how to protect his earnings.

I felt very fortunate to have had Richard and Wayne involved in Malcolm's career. There are many business managers out there and although some are just as stellar as Wayne and Richard, some are not. Over the years, there have been many high-profile scandals dealing with crooked business managers. It is up to you to do your homework to find the right fit for your child's finances.

Unfortunately for us, after 30 years, Wayne Mejia is retiring, and I have had to move the business to another firm. It was terrifying. A thirty-year relationship that Malcolm and I have depended on, was now having to be dissolved. Once again, research was very critical. How do you move a 30-year-old financial entity to a place of safety where there is no relationship and trust has not been established? It was my responsibility to make that happen.

Through research, referrals and vetting by financial institutions, we are now with the firm Mann Gelon Glodney Gumerove Yee.

CHAPTER 7

THE ATTORNEY

Another vital player in your showbiz kid's career is the attorney. It is very important to have an experienced attorney. The attorney you choose should be one who primarily works in the field of entertainment law. Just as you would not go to a heart doctor for a broken leg, you want an attorney who specifically works in entertainment. Entertainment contracts are different from other contracts. The entertainment attorney brings invaluable expertise to the table. A contract is a binding document that you must uphold, or you and your child can be sued. Lawsuits are very costly in both time and money and can tie you up in court for a very long time, which would negatively affect your showbiz kid's ability to work. Avoid a lawsuit whenever possible!

A good attorney will make sure the contract you sign will be one you will be able to uphold. An entertainment attorney is an expert at putting all the moving parts together. He or she understands the workings of the production companies, the production executives, studios, and other attorneys who may be involved in a negotiation. Sometimes they may have relationships with these other entities that may work in your child's favor. It's always easier to negotiate with a friend than a stranger.

Additionally, there is an art to structuring a deal. Barry Haldeman, who had been Malcolm's attorney for 25 years, is an artist in deal making.

Barry has headed up production studios, and knows the ins and outs of making a deal. He has been the lead attorney at several high-profile law firms and has been our go-to person for all legal matters in entertainment. The deals that he has structured for Malcolm have been phenomenal. Those deals have provided the foundation from which Malcolm has grown as an artist and businessman.

Currently, Malcolm is represented by John Meigs, a heavy hitter in all aspects of the entertainment industry. John is a Harvard Law graduate and a partner at Hansen Jacobson Teller Hoberman et al. John has structured deals for Malcolm that have greatly advanced and enhanced his career.

Once again, you must do your research. There are good attorneys out there and some who are not so good. Finding the right person will always be a journey. The good thing is that it is not a lifetime commitment. If you are not comfortable with an attorney, business manager, agent, or manager, you can always make a change until you find the right person for you and your child.

CHAPTER 8

THE PUBLICIST

The publicist's job is to keep the actor in front of the public. The other part of the job is to create opportunities for the actor. They spread the word about the actor and the current project or show the actor is working on. The publicist is another vital component in the career of the actor. However, it is not necessary to hire a publicist until you have something to promote. They need material and information to do their jobs effectively. Their job is to tell a story about the actor. If your showbiz kid is not working on a project, you don't really need to hire one.

If your child is on a show, normally the show itself will have a publicist for the promotion of that show. There will be some attention given to the cast, however the job of the show publicist is only to promote the show. An actor may want to have a personal publicist whose sole focus is on the actor. The publicity that the publicist generates helps to create a strong fan base. The publicist also creates an awareness within the entertainment industry. The casting directors, writers, producers, and directors are always looking for and interested in a fresh new face. The publicist's job is to get that fresh new face in front of the public.

While the publicist is a logical addition to your team, he or she can be costly. Fees for a publicist can range anywhere between $2,500-$6,000 each month. Some PR firms require a minimum three-month commitment and some as long as six months. Public relation firms understand that child actors may have limited budgets. They can offer per event services as opposed to the three to six-month commitment. But you will have to Google and do research to find a publicist who understands the needs of the child actor who is just starting out.

You will need to determine when is the best time to bring a publicist on board. Your manager can help you with this decision. If your showbiz kid only has a few lines in a film, this may not be the best time to hire a PR person. However, if she or he is the lead in a series, lead in a film, or has a recurring role, perhaps it may be a good idea.

Once again, we were fortunate in this area. We were introduced to a wonderful young woman, Jordyn Palos, who was making great strides in the public relations arena. Her company, Persona PR, was young and thriving. It is now one of the top public relations firms in the entertainment industry. With offices in Los Angeles and New York, Jordyn has positioned her company to be a leader in traditional and digital public relations campaigns, both nationally and internationally. Her client base includes a number of A-list actors, directors, producers, musicians, and content creators.

One of the many aspects of her firm that was attractive to Malcolm and me was that the account could go on hiatus when there was downtime or projects had been completed. There was no ongoing billing when projects had been completed or when there was nothing to promote. When Malcolm needs coverage, she is all over it. From Los Angeles to New York, she gets his image out in front of the public. And she is an absolute pleasure to work with.

CHAPTER 9

YOU ARE THE TEAM CAPTAIN

You now have the basic moving parts assembled. You have created a team for your showbiz kid. It is now up to you, the team captain, to decide how to manage the team. Do you want to delegate from the sidelines, or do you want to be as hands-on as possible? The other team members know their jobs. But, as with any team, there needs to be leadership and goals set. What is your vision, and what goals do you have for your child? This is something to discuss with your team members. Everyone needs to be on the same page.

You are all working toward one goal, and that is to have a happy, healthy, and successful showbiz kid.

I chose to be hands-on. I regularly interfaced with the agents, business manager, and publicist. I was the team leader, and I took the responsibility to keep all the components moving smoothly.

For more than 30 years, I was the team captain. Everything ran smoothly, and Malcolm did well. The industry was changing rapidly, and I began to see the need to bring on another member of the team for fresh new energy and ideas. I decided to co-manage. I hired Adam Griffin, who was a partner at Link Entertainment at the time. Adam has moved on and now heads his own management firm, Vault Entertainment. It was one of the best decisions I made. Adam is a dynamic young man who brought enthusiasm, shared my vision for Malcolm's career, and provided the support I needed. And I got promoted to Chief of Staff.

Co-managing is quite common and something you may wish to explore. As a person new to the industry, a co-management situation might work well for you. It will give you the opportunity to learn from an established professional, and you won't be doing all the heavy lifting alone. Not all managers will want to do this due to the issue of splitting fees, but it certainly won't hurt to explore the possibility.

CHAPTER 10

THE COOGAN LAW

The Coogan Law is named after the actor Jackie Coogan, who became a very successful child actor from the 1920s through the 1930s. By the time Jackie Coogan turned 21, he found he had nothing left of his estimated $4 million in earnings. His mother and stepfather had squandered his money. He sued them and was able to recover, after legal fees, approximately $126,000. Macaulay Culkin, Gary Coleman, Mischa Barton, and Le Ann Rimes are among child-actors-turned-adults who have taken their parents to court over the mishandling, mismanagement, and theft of their earnings as child actors.

The Coogan Law was designed to protect the earnings of child actors. This law requires that 15 percent of the child's earnings be placed in what is called a blocked trust. This is a requirement in the states of California, New York, New Mexico, and Louisiana. The purpose of this account is to set aside a portion of the earnings for the child until they turn 18. This account is the recipient of the child's earnings.

There can be no withdrawals from this account until the child has reached the age of 18. This is to protect the earnings of the child from mismanagement and possible squandering by the child's parents.

California is very strict with this law. When presenting your child's work permit to a production company, you will also be required to show proof that this account has been opened. It is also a requirement that if you are working in the state of California, the account must be opened in a California bank, regardless of where you may reside.

In New York, Louisiana, and New Mexico, the trust account isn't called a Coogan account. It is titled the Uniform Transfer to Minors Act (UTMA) or Uniform Gift to Minors Act (UGMA). These accounts, unlike in California, can be opened in any bank in any state. For states other than New York, California, New Mexico, and Louisiana, I recommend you contact the local labor board for the laws that govern the employment of minors in those particular states.

CHAPTER 11

THE UNION IS YOUR FRIEND

The union, as in other industries, is created to protect workers and to ensure fair wages and safe working environments for its members.

The union that covers the entertainment industry is titled Screen Actors Guild and the American Federation of Television and Radio Artists (SAG-AFTRA). SAG was formed in 1933. AFTRA was formed in 1937. Actors' Equity Association (AEA), also referred to as Equity, was formed in 1913.

Originally, these were separate unions and covered different aspects of the industry. SAG covered actors in motion pictures, television shows, and commercials that were recorded on film. AFTRA covered actors in television and commercials that were live productions or productions recorded on audio or videotape. This also included disc jockeys, news reporters, radio performers, and announcers. AEA covered theatrical productions. On March 30, 2012, SAG and AFTRA merged. With this merger, SAG-AFTRA now represents over 160,000 film and television actors and other media professionals.

Being a member of the union provides protection and support for your child. There are non-union acting jobs, but with these you will be taking a risk. If there is a problem with a non-union job, there is little recourse. With the union, you can lodge your complaint and get support in rectifying issues that may arise. Also, with the union, minimum salaries are regulated, but with non-union jobs, there is less oversight. If you are not a union member, you can work non-union jobs. But once you become a union member, you are ineligible to work non-union-acting jobs. There are union actors who do accept non-union jobs; however, there are penalties for doing so.

There are differing schools of thought on having your showbiz kid join the union. With non-union jobs, your child has the opportunity to gain experience and build a resume. Often, it may be easier to book non-union jobs when you are just starting out. While investigating and searching for an agent and manager, non-union jobs can get your child in front of casting directors. However, these jobs pay less and have fewer regulations. Non-union jobs can take advantage, as they are not closely regulated. The work hours can be longer, and liberties can be taken as it relates to the on-set tutoring of your child, the length of time the child is on set, breaks, etc. Non-union jobs can take up to 60 days before they pay.

Union membership can be costly. The initiation fee to join SAG-AFTRA is $3,000 and yearly dues are based on income. So being non-union can have its benefits for a while. Eventually, your child must join, and cannot work unless they join the union.

By being a union member, the child is best protected. Under union laws and regulations, the time a child can be on set, the number of mandatory breaks the child must have, and tutoring are strictly regulated. When a child works for a consecutive number of days, an on-set tutor is mandatory and is provided by the production company. If there are any problems or conflicts, the union representatives will work diligently to solve those problems and bring about a resolution. The union works for you. In addition, earnings from jobs are paid in a timely manner and regulated by the union. Also, the rates of pay are regulated.

Once again, do your research. Have conversations with other parents who have showbiz kids. Call the union and meet with a representative who will give you more detailed information to help you make the right decision for you and your child.

CHAPTER 12

WHEN YOU ARE ON THE SET

Being on the set with your showbiz kid can entail long hours of you just doing nothing. While your focus is on your child, I admit it can be boring. My suggestion is to bring a good book, knitting, your laptop, or something that will keep you busy while your child is working.

Under these circumstances, it is very easy to engage in conversations with the crew or the cast. One mistake that many parents make is to get overly chatty. Remember, these are working people and not your newfound BFFs.

It is wise not to get so comfortable that you are discussing your personal life and challenges. And it is absolutely not acceptable to discuss whatever issues you may have with production. That is a conversation for you to have with your agent and/or manager. If you have not formed a team, the union representative can handle your complaints. If you are displeased with the working conditions, the call times, the script, or anything at all, on set is definitely not the place to vent to the cast or crew. Believe me, your venting and dissatisfaction will go straight to the producers, and that will not be good for you or your child.

Your behavior as the manager-parent and how you interact with those around you, can have an adverse or positive effect on your child's career. Remember, you are there to take care of your child, not to become Ms./Mr. Popularity. On the other hand, if you tend to cause problems, behave in a nonprofessional way, are disruptive, pushy, and confrontational, that will become your reputation. If you show up as a professional, are friendly and cooperative, are on time with your child, ready and prepared to work, that also builds your reputation as a professional. Be clear that your behavior as a parent who manages will follow you and can have positive as well as negative effects on your child's ability to get hired. Things can be pretty fluid on set and, believe me, the word will get around.

Because I put together a team for Malcolm early on, I played what I call "kissy huggy politics". I had wonderful relationships with the director and producers of *The Cosby Show*. If there were problems that needed to be addressed, or if there were active contract negotiations underway or any changes that were needed, I never confronted the producers. I left that totally up to the agent and lawyer. My attitude was all kissy, huggy, sweetness, and light. But behind the scenes, with my team, I addressed what was needed and left them to do the heavy lifting. That was their job. My job was to be the face of professionalism.

Keep in mind that while your showbiz kid is wonderful and brilliant and just a remarkable young talent, your child was hired for a specific reason. It may be a look; it could be as simple as your child's height or those cute freckles, and of course, your child's talent. But always keep in mind that this is a job, and your child can be replaced. It's very similar to being in any industry. There is a need for a certain skill and those with that skill will be hired. Your child was hired to fill a role that the script required.

I know this may be a hard one for some parents. Even if you are certain that your showbiz kid is the most wonderful talent that ever walked the earth, just keep in mind that your child is among thousands of the most wonderful and talented kids that have ever walked the earth. This is about perspective. This is about being realistic and pacing your child's career. If this is what you and your child have decided as a lifelong career choice, then there will be more than enough time to show the world that your showbiz kid is a star and that you are a competent parent/manager.

CHAPTER 13

YOU ARE NOT A MOMAGER

Unfortunately, parents who manage their children have gotten a bad rap. As long as there has been show business, there have been stage mothers and fathers. Anxious, obnoxious, and pushy parents have created the image that agents, managers, producers, and directors have in their minds. Although parents can be a total nightmare, some of their behavior is a result of their fear and not understanding the process. And some are those parents I wrote about earlier: parents with unmet needs living through their children.

The last thing you want to do is to reinforce that negative perception through your behavior or title. If you are calling yourself a momager, you are doing yourself a huge disservice. Through no fault of your own, you come to the table as a parent who manages with historical disadvantages. It is understood that you are the parent. Your position does not need to be reinforced with the title momager. You are a professional; you are a manager, period!

I worked very hard to be as professional as I possibly could be. I was fully aware of the history of parents who have managed badly. In meetings, I would never allow my son to refer to me as anything other than Mrs. Warner or "my manager." It is about establishing respect and sending the message that you are indeed a professional and that you come to the table to do business. Referring to yourself as a momager, in my estimation, takes away from that.

And let us not forget that fathers also manage their children. What would you call a father who manages? A dadager? It's silly and has no place in a professional setting. You don't want anything to take away your power. You want to be taken seriously and be respected for the professional that you are.

While you cannot undo the history of hysterical, obnoxious, and pushy parents, you can be part of re-writing that history by how you handle yourself as a parent who manages. It is important to be informed by doing your research and obtaining as much information as you can about how this business works. By understanding that this is a business and should be taken seriously, you are not only a parent, but you are also an entertainment professional who manages your showbiz kid's career.

You want to be the parent with whom producers and directors want to work with. Not the parent for whom they have to steel themselves when you arrive on set because they know you will be a problem. Remember, you are building your reputation and the reputation of your showbiz kid. Both are precious and must be handled with great care.

CHAPTER 14

THE GREEN BLUES

The Green Blues is a condition that is not uncommon in many families and among friends. It becomes particularly prominent once you've entered the world of show business.

There is a perception that anyone on television is automatically rich. Many people outside this business think that being on either television or in a film, no matter how small the role, catapults people into the financial stratosphere. Things couldn't be further from the truth.

Depending on the financial history of a family, the paychecks can be an amount that most families have never seen at one time. And this can be very exciting initially. But then reality sets in. The bigger the check, the larger the taxes that must be paid. Remember, the IRS will come after your child just like they will come after you for non-payment. In addition, you must contribute to a mandatory fund of some sort. Either a Coogan account or a blocked account, as discussed in Chapter 10. Then, there are expenses that must be made toward the care of your client. So that wonderful check soon starts diminishing quickly.

While money is not the root of all evil, sometimes it can make things very difficult. The difficult part is saying no to family and friends who may now perceive you as being rich and that you can easily afford to make loans. Let's face it: family is family. You, of course, want to help. But you can't help with your child's hard-earned money. If you wish to help, it must be from your own funds. It can be very difficult to say no. But you must. You will be vilified; you will be accused of being selfish. You will be castigated and made to feel ashamed for not accommodating their needs. But remember, there is no entitlement here. Your child's success is your child's success, not Uncle Bob or Aunt Mildred, nor your brother or sister, mama, or daddy. Also, keep in mind that you are totally responsible for any mishandling of your child's money. You may lose a family member or two and even a friend or two because you said no! It is one of the more difficult parts of the job of managing a showbiz kid. It may help if you develop a standard response to stop the asking. The most basic being: "No, I can't."

Just remember, your responsibility is to take care and safeguard your child's career and finances. This is the part that can be hard. Keep your focus on doing what is right for your child. At the end of the day, you will be okay.

CHAPTER 15

STRANGER DANGER

The relationship between an agent and talent is one built on trust and dependence. It is a reasonable expectation that you can trust the person chosen to guide your career. And you depend on them to make sure you are a working actor, and that they are seeking out the jobs that will keep you a working actor. The expectations are the same for the child actor.

Unfortunately, that trust can and has been broken. It is always regrettable on any level, but when it happens to a vulnerable child, it is particularly vile.

Many of us assume that people in positions of power come with some sort of halo and we assume that these people are good based on nothing more than their title: doctor, lawyer, teacher, talent agent, etc. It is assumed they are mentally healthy and have your best interests at heart. Often, this is just not true. As the manager of an underage and vulnerable child, you must be particularly careful in dealing with the agent and your child actor.

In dealing with an agent and your child, you are the first line of contact. I believe the agent must respect your dual position as manager and parent. Conversations should always be between you and the agent. You are the manager, and you can relay all important information to your child. Or you can do three-way calls, or with modern technology you can Zoom! There should never be "private" conversations between your child and the agent or manager.

It is your right and responsibility to be front and center of the interaction and relationship with the agent. You must be present at all times. This protects your client as their manager, and your child as their parent. The internet is rife with examples of abuse by talent agents and managers. Sadly, there are many cases of sexual exploitation and sexual abuse of children and teens in this industry. Once again, do your research. If something does not feel right, trust your gut/ intuition. If your child is not comfortable with the agent or the manager, listen to your child and make whatever changes you may need to make immediately. It is far more important that your child is safe than the next job!

CHAPTER 16

THE EMANCIPATED MINOR

This is a really tough one. I've included this chapter so that you are aware this is a situation you would want to avoid at all costs.

An emancipated minor is a child who is legally independent of their parents.

A minor child who petitions for emancipation is usually a child in crisis. It is not easy to become an emancipated minor, and it is usually done as a last resort. Minors in show business who seek emancipation from their parents do so under great duress. Some of the reasons can be due to physical and mental abuse by a parent, a parent's inability to protect the financial interests of the child, or a parent's gross mismanagement of the child's career. Sometimes emancipation is sought to skirt the child labor laws, which are rather strict but are for the protection of the child and to prevent the abuse of the child actor.

There are many high-profile child actors who have gone to court to become emancipated. Macaulay Culkin, Drew Barrymore, Michelle Williams, and Alicia Silverstone are a few high-profile child actors who successfully emancipated from their parents.

For me, it gets back to your relationship with your child. Is there clear communication between the two of you? Does your child feel safe with how you are managing or with the team of agents and managers that you have assembled? If there are issues, are you able to work out those issues and come to a resolution? These are questions that only you can answer. These are also questions that may need to be reviewed with your child/client from time to time. Check in with your child/client often.

The primary goal in all of this is to have a successful, happy, and thriving showbiz kid. It is also to have a healthy working relationship that thrives and grows into success for your showbiz kid and for you as well.

Every child is different. There is no one-size-fits-all way of managing. This is a trial-and-error endeavor. You will make mistakes, but you will also have successes. Always trust your gut and always aim to do the right thing for your showbiz kid.

CONCLUSION

As you embark on this journey, it is understandable that you will be afraid. You will make mistakes, which will be part of your learning experience as a parent who manages his or her showbiz kid. There is so much to learn and experience. You are not yet an expert, but you are on your way to becoming one. This will be an adventure for you and your showbiz kid, and hopefully it will be a pleasant one. While there is so much to consider, as long as your child's welfare and well-being are your focus and your goal, you will do very well.

Again, I cannot emphasize this enough. Always do your research. This is very important. Remember, knowledge is power. Also, keep in mind that you are the very best person for this job. You know your child better than anyone. You know what your child needs, wants, and desires. Whether you take the reins yourself or hire a team, you are still in control and you will always have the last word when it comes to the welfare of your minor child.

Remember, don't be afraid to ask questions. Ask questions until you have the answers. Don't feel foolish because you may be asking the same questions again and again. Ask until you have the answers and understanding that you need in order to make the best decisions for your showbiz kid.

I have thoroughly enjoyed my life as a parent who managed a showbiz kid, even though it was frightening and exhilarating all at the same time. I enjoyed the learning process and embraced my mistakes, along with my successes. I am very fortunate to still be in the role of managing my son's career, even though now he is a mature adult. It has been a long journey, but we have both survived and thrived. And you will as well.

It is with much gratitude that I am able to share my journey with you. I sincerely hope you have gained some insights and information that will help you on your journey to successfully manage your showbiz kid.

GLOSSARY OF TERMS[1]

AGENT

An agent is a person whose primary function is to secure work for his/her clients. The agent functions as a salesperson and sells the talent of the person being represented. In exchange for finding work, the agent is paid an agreed-upon commission, which is usually 10 percent of monies earned. This figure can be negotiated, but the industry norm for an agent is 10 percent.

ART DEPARTMENT

This department executes the vision of the production designer in creating the look of the film or television show.

1 Definitions from the following sources: 1) Levy, F. (2009, January 1). *Acting in Young Hollywood*. Back Stage Books; 2) Padol, B. A., & Simon, A. (1990, January 1). *The Young Performer's Guide*. Betterway Book; and 3) Pamela Warner from her 40 years of professional experience.

ASSISTANT DIRECTOR

This is a crew member responsible for delegating the director's instructions and making sure the cast and crew are in their required places at the right time.

ATMOSPHERE

Extras in a scene who fill up the space surrounding the principal actors to make the scene look real or believable.

AUDITION

An opportunity to try out for a television or film role, usually for a casting director. It is a meeting held between a casting director and an actor in which the actor demonstrates his/her talent, and the casting director can assess if that actor is right for the role. Auditions are highly competitive and stressful for both the child and adult actor.

AVAIL

On avail is a designation for an actor who is being considered for a role. The actor on avail must notify the production company if another role is offered.

BILLING

The order and placement of names at the opening of a film or television show.

BLOCKING

The physical movement by actors in a scene. During the early stages of rehearsal in either a play, film, or television show, the director will work with the actors to plan specific onstage movements and positioning. This process is done with focused attention on detail and works slowly from line to line.

BOOKING

When an actor is hired for a role. This is a firm commitment for a specific role in a production.

BREAKDOWN

A detailed listing of current casting roles.

CALL BACK

A follow-up interview or audition for an actor being considered for a role in film, television, theater, or television.

CALL SHEET

Lists the schedule of scenes to be shot, the length of each scene, the cast members who need to report to work that day, and the time that each member of the crew needs to report to the set.

CASTING DIRECTOR

A person hired by the producer who is responsible for selecting lead and supporting actors for film, television, or theater.

CASTING EXECUTIVE

An executive on the studio or network level who supervises the casting of all projects for the studio or network.

COLD READING

The unrehearsed reading of a scene at an audition.

COMMISSION

The percentage of an actor's earnings paid to a manager or agent for services rendered. For agents, the amount is 10 percent. For managers, this number can vary depending on the agreement between the manager and actor. The industry standard is 15 percent.

COPY
The printed material or script used for a film, commercial, or television series.

COOGAN ACCOUNT
A blocked trust account that is required to get a work permit for a minor. These accounts are created to set aside 15 percent of a child's earnings until the child turns 18.

CO-STAR
A leading actor or actress appearing in a movie, on stage, or in a television show with another actor or actors of equal importance.

CRAFT SERVICES
Members of the crew who are responsible for providing meals to the cast and crew

CREW
All technicians, production assistants, Directors Guild of America (DGA) trainees, prop people, costume designers, teamsters, assistant directors, tutors, nurses, gaffers, best boys, carpenters, electricians, and engineers are all people who work behind the camera and who are responsible for making the movie or television show.

COSTUMER
Crew member who is responsible for the wardrobe for film, television, and theater.

CUE
Hand signal given by an assistant director or stage manager.

DAY PLAYER
An actor hired and paid to work on a daily basis as opposed to a long-term contract.

DEAL MEMO
A short-form agreement outlining the major terms of a deal prior to a long-form contract.

DEMO
An audition reel is a montage of carefully selected and edited scenes of an actor's work as a performer in film and television. Demo reels are typically one or two minutes in length. The demo reel is generally submitted along with a resume to casting directors, producers, and directors when seeking employment.

DEVELOPMENT EXECUTIVE
A studio or network executive who finds and develops new projects.

DIALOGUE
The words in a script exchanged by actors.

DIRECTOR
The primary creative and artistic force behind a film or television show in charge of the actors' performance on camera and determining the overall look and feel of the film or television show.

EMANCIPATED MINOR

An emancipated minor is a child who has been granted the status of adulthood by a court order or other formal agreement, and who has demonstrated the ability to be financially independent.

EPISODIC

A television series that consists of multiple episodes/shows.

EXECUTIVE PRODUCER

The person responsible for funding the film production. In television, the executive producer is the head writer of the show.

EXTRA

A background actor who has no lines.

FEATURE

A motion picture or film.

FRANCHISED AGENT

An agent approved by SAG-AFTRA to solicit work for clients.

GENERAL MEETING

A meeting for a casting director or agent to get to know an actor better.

GUARANTEED BILLING

A position of credit negotiated by an agent prior to signing a contract.

GUEST STAR
A large guest role on a television show.

HEADSHOT
An 8x10 still photograph of the actor that is considered the actors' business card and is sent out to casting offices for the purpose of securing auditions.

HONEY WAGON
The smallest-sized trailer/dressing room with no frills that actors use.

INDUSTRIAL
Non-broadcast film that is presented to distributors, dealers, and others to sell products or services.

LOCAL HIRE
An actor who is hired locally, thereby eliminating travel, housing, or per diem costs for the production company.

MAIN TITLES
The credit sequence that appears at the beginning of a film or television show, or in cases where there are no opening credits at the beginning of a film or television show, the credit sequence that immediately follows a movie.

MANAGER
A professional representative whose primary function is to guide and advise a performer's career. A manager assists the actor in developing the overall image and making career choices, and handles the business affairs of the actor. The commissions for managers is 10 percent.

MEAL PENALTY
A fine imposed on a production if a meal isn't served within six hours of call time or from the previous meal.

NON-UNION
An actor who is not a member of SAG-AFTRA or AE.

OFF BOOK
When an actor does not need to rely on his material/script for an audition.

OPEN CALL
An audition that is open to everyone, also referred to as a cattle call.

PER DIEM
Money given to an actor to cover incidental expenses while filming on location.

PLUS TEN
An agent's commission that is often negotiated into deals (that are scaled) so the actor doesn't have to deduct that commission from his salary.

POST PRODUCTION
Term used for all stages of production after completion of principal photography.

PREPRODUCTION
Everything that takes place before filming.

PRIME TIME
Network programming aired between 8pm and 11pm.

PRINCIPAL
A performer with speaking lines or special business that advances the story line.

PRODUCER
The person who is ultimately responsible for the success or failure of a film and who generally oversees a project from initial concepts through release. The producer is responsible on a daily basis for the decision-making process involved in a production. In television, the producers are the writers who ultimately guide the vision of the series.

PRODUCTION MANAGER
Person responsible for the day-to-day oversight of the production.

PROGRAMMING EXECUTIVE
The studio or network executive who supervises current television programs.

PUBLICIST
A person who is responsible for generating press and media coverage for an actor.

RATINGS
Public surveys used to determine the percentage of listening or viewing audiences for radio and television.

REHEARSAL
The activity wherein the actors, technicians, dancers, musicians, and everyone else involved in a production study their lines, run through their blocking, and practice their technical cues; all in preparation for a public presentation.

RESIDUAL
A fee paid to a performer for the reuse of a commercial, film, or television show.

RESUME
A listing of work experience or credits.

SCALE
The least, or minimum, amount paid for a job.

SCREEN TEST
The filming of an audition on tape.

SCRIPT
The written form of a screenplay for film or television.

SERIES REGULAR
An actor who is part of the main cast of a television series.

SESSION FEE
Payment for the initial performance in a commercial.

SET
An indoor location, usually within a studio.

SHOWCASE

A performance by an artist attended by industry professionals for the purpose of obtaining an agent, manager, record deal, etc.

SIDES

A scene or pages from a script containing only the lines and cues of a specific actor's role, which is used for auditions.

SIGHT AND SOUND

The right of a parent under union contract to be within sight of their child at all times.

STAND-IN

A person, other than the actor, who is used to block and light a scene that involves that actor.

STUDIO TEACHER

A teacher or tutor hired by the studio to teach minors and to enforce child labor laws under the guidelines of union contracts.

SUBMISSION

Performers selected by an agent for a casting director's consideration for a particular role.

TABLE READ

When the entire cast of actors reads the script out loud, enabling the writers and producers to hear how their words sound so that changes can be made if necessary.

TAFT-HARTLEY
The process by which a non-union actor is allowed to work in a film or television show, thereby making the actor eligible to join the union.

TEST
An audition before studio and/or network executives.

TEST DEAL
A pre-negotiated agreement that is set prior to an actor testing for a film or television series.

THEATRICAL AGENT
An agent who represents talent for film and television.

TOP OF SHOW
The largest guest star role on an episodic television show.

TRAILER
A series of clips used to promote a film or television show.

TURN AROUND TIME
The period between when a production wraps and when they begin again the next day. Union rules specify at least 12 hours of turnaround time.

VOICE OVER AGENT
An agent who represents talent for radio ads and animation.

WARDROBE
The clothing a performer wears in front of the camera.

WARDROBE FITTING

A paid session prior to the shoot used to select clothing the actor will wear.

WORK PERMIT

A legal document that allows minors to work in the entertainment industry.

WORK SESSION

An opportunity for an actor to work one-on-one with the director or casting director before an audition or test.

WRAP

The wrap is announced when production ends for the day or when the shooting of a project is finished in its entirety.

ABOUT THE AUTHOR

Pamela Warner has been an entrepreneur most of her life. Her first entrepreneurial project began after graduation from college. Unable to find employment in her field, she launched Ms. Goodcookie. This catering business was the precursor to the movable feast that serviced small mom-and-pop businesses along the Crenshaw Blvd. corridor—predating the fast-food restaurants now dominating that area.

Around the same time her son's career began flourishing, she was thrust into full-time management. Without any training and little guidance, Pamela successfully guided her son's career to its current success.

In 1994, she established Warner Management, a multi-faceted management company involved in producing and guiding its clients' careers. Warner Management provides a conduit and platform for artistic expression.

In 2013, Showbiz Consulting 411 was launched to assist, inform, and prepare parents interested in being a part of the entertainment industry.

Pamela Warner is a graduate of California State University at Los Angeles and holds a BA in Speech Communications.

You may reach her at showbizconsulting411@gmail.com or showbizconsulting411.com.

Pamela Warner and Malcolm-Jamal Warner

Notes

NOTES

NOTES

Made in the USA
Middletown, DE
24 February 2024

49803274R00057